Christmas Cookies

CLASSIC RECIPES™

Publications International, Ltd.
Favorite Brand Name Recipes at www.fbnr.com

Microwave Cooking: Microwave ovens vary in wattage. Use the cooking times as guidelines and check for doneness before adding more time.

Preparation/Cooking Times: Preparation times are based on the approximate amount of time required to assemble the recipe before cooking, baking, chilling or serving. These times include preparation steps such as measuring, chopping and mixing. The fact that some preparations and cooking can be done simultaneously is taken into account. Preparation of optional ingredients and serving suggestions are not included.

Table of Contents

Kris Kringle's Cut-Outs

Gingerbread People and Holiday Sugar Cookies (page 74)

Now's your chance to get in on the best Christmas has to offer and enjoy some of Santa's personal favorites. These cut-out cookies will help you spread the holiday spirit.

Gingerbread People

$^1/_2$ cup butter, softened
$^1/_2$ cup packed brown sugar
$^1/_3$ cup molasses
$^1/_3$ cup water
1 egg
4 cups all-purpose flour
2 teaspoons baking soda
1 teaspoon ground ginger
$^1/_2$ teaspoon ground allspice
$^1/_2$ teaspoon ground cinnamon
$^1/_2$ teaspoon ground cloves
White or colored frostings

Beat butter and brown sugar in large bowl at medium speed of electric mixer until creamy. Add molasses, water and egg; beat until blended. Stir in flour, baking soda, ginger, allspice, cinnamon and cloves until well blended. Cover; refrigerate about 2 hours or until firm.

Preheat oven to 350°F. Grease cookie sheets. Roll out dough to $^1/_8$-inch thickness on lightly floured surface with lightly floured rolling pin. Cut with cookie cutter. Place 2 inches apart on prepared cookie sheets.

Bake 12 to 15 minutes or until firm to the touch. Cool 1 minute on cookie sheets. Remove to wire racks; cool completely. Decorate with frostings. Store in airtight containers.   *Makes about 4$^1/_2$ dozen cookies*

Christmas Ornament Cookies

2$\frac{1}{4}$ cups all-purpose flour
$\frac{1}{4}$ teaspoon salt
1 cup sugar
$\frac{3}{4}$ cup butter, softened
1 large egg
1 teaspoon vanilla
1 teaspoon almond extract
Icing (recipe follows)
Assorted candies and decors

Place flour and salt in medium bowl; stir to combine. Beat sugar and butter in large bowl with electric mixer at medium speed until light and fluffy. Beat in egg, vanilla and almond extract. Gradually add flour mixture. Beat at low speed until well blended. Divide dough in half; cover and refrigerate 30 minutes or until firm.

Preheat oven to 350°F. Working with 1 portion at a time, roll out dough on lightly floured surface to $\frac{1}{4}$-inch thickness. Cut dough into desired shapes with assorted floured cookie cutters. Reroll trimmings and cut out more cookies. Place cutouts on ungreased baking sheets. Using drinking straw or tip of sharp knife, cut hole near top of each cookie to allow for piece of ribbon or string to be inserted for hanger. Bake 10 to 12 minutes or until edges are golden brown. Let cookies stand on baking sheets 1 minute. Remove cookies to wire racks; cool completely.

Prepare Icing. Spoon Icing into small resealable plastic food storage bag. Cut off very tiny corner of bag; pipe Icing decoratively on cookies. Decorate with candies as desired. Let stand at room temperature 40 minutes or until set. Thread ribbon through each cookie hole to hang as Christmas tree ornaments. *Makes about 2 dozen cookies*

Icing

> 2 cups powdered sugar
> 2 tablespoons milk or lemon juice
> Food coloring (optional)

Place powdered sugar and milk in small bowl; stir with spoon until smooth. (Icing will be very thick. If it is too thick, stir in 1 teaspoon additional milk.) Divide into small bowls and tint with food coloring, if desired.

Christmas Ornament Cookies

Chocolate Reindeer

1 cup butter, softened
1 cup granulated sugar
1 egg
1 teaspoon vanilla
2 ounces semisweet chocolate, melted
2¼ cups all-purpose flour
1 teaspoon baking powder
¼ teaspoon salt
    Royal Icing (recipe follows)
    Assorted food colors
    Assorted small candies

1. Beat butter and sugar in large bowl at high speed of electric mixer until fluffy. Beat in egg and vanilla. Add melted chocolate; mix well. Add flour, baking powder and salt; mix well. Divide dough in half; wrap each half in plastic wrap and refrigerate 2 hours or until firm.

2. Preheat oven to 325°F. Grease 2 cookie sheets; set aside.

3. Roll one half of dough on well-floured surface to ¼-inch thickness. Cut out with reindeer cookie cutter. Place 2 inches apart on prepared cookie sheets. Chill 10 minutes.

4. Bake 13 to 15 minutes or until set. Cool completely on cookie sheets. Repeat steps with remaining dough.

5. Prepare Royal Icing. Tint with food colors as desired. Pipe icing on reindeer and decorate with small candies. For best results, let cookies dry overnight uncovered before storing in airtight container at room temperature. *Makes 10 (4-inch) cookies*

Royal Icing

2 to 3 large egg whites*
2 to 4 cups powdered sugar
1 tablespoon lemon juice
    Assorted food colors

*Use only grade A clean, uncracked eggs.

Beat 2 egg whites in medium bowl with electric mixer until peaks just
begin to hold their shape. Add 2 cups powdered sugar and lemon juice;
beat for 1 minute. If consistency is too thin for piping, gradually add more
sugar until desired result is achieved; if it is too thick, add another egg
white. Divide icing among several small bowls and tint to desired colors.
Keep bowls tightly covered until ready to use.

Chocolate Reindeer

Holiday Wreath Cookies

1 package (20 ounces) refrigerated sugar cookie dough
2 cups shredded coconut
2 to 3 drops green food color
1 container (16 ounces) French vanilla frosting
   Green sugar or small cinnamon candies

1. Preheat oven to 350°F. Remove dough from wrapper according to package directions. Divide dough in half; wrap half of dough in plastic wrap and refrigerate. Roll out remaining half of dough on well-floured surface to ⅛-inch thickness. Cut with cookie cutters to resemble wreaths. Repeat with remaining half of dough.

2. Place cookies about 2 inches apart on ungreased baking sheets. Bake 7 to 9 minutes or until edges are lightly browned. Remove cookies from baking sheets to wire racks to cool completely.

3. Place coconut in resealable plastic food storage bag. Add food color; seal bag and shake until coconut is evenly tinted. Frost cookies with frosting and decorate with coconut, green sugar and cinnamon candies.

Makes about 2 dozen cookies

Prep and Bake Time: 30 minutes

Holiday Wreath Cookies

Jolly Peanut Butter Gingerbread Cookies

1 2/3 cups (10-ounce package) REESE'S® Peanut Butter Chips
3/4 cup (1 1/2 sticks) butter or margarine, softened
1 cup packed light brown sugar
1 cup dark corn syrup
2 eggs
5 cups all-purpose flour
1 teaspoon baking soda
1/2 teaspoon ground cinnamon
1/4 teaspoon ground ginger
1/4 teaspoon salt

1. Place peanut butter chips in small microwave-safe bowl. Microwave at HIGH (100%) 1 to 2 minutes or until chips are melted when stirred. Beat melted peanut butter chips and butter in large bowl until well blended. Add brown sugar, corn syrup and eggs; beat until fluffy.

2. Stir together flour, baking soda, cinnamon, ginger and salt. Add half of flour mixture to butter mixture; beat on low speed of mixer until smooth. With wooden spoon, stir in remaining flour mixture until well blended. Divide into thirds; wrap each in plastic wrap. Refrigerate at least 1 hour or until dough is firm enough to roll.

3. Heat oven to 325°F. Roll 1 dough portion at a time to 1/8-inch thickness on lightly floured surface; with floured cookie cutters, cut into holiday shapes. Place on ungreased cookie sheet.

4. Bake 10 to 12 minutes or until set and lightly browned. Cool slightly; remove from cookie sheet to wire rack. Cool completely. Frost and decorate as desired.   *Makes about 6 dozen cookies*

Jolly Peanut Butter Gingerbread Cookies

Peanut Butter Bears

1 cup SKIPPY® Creamy Peanut Butter
1 cup (2 sticks) margarine or butter, softened
1 cup packed brown sugar
2/3 cup KARO® Light or Dark Corn Syrup
2 eggs
4 cups flour, divided
1 tablespoon baking powder
1 teaspoon cinnamon (optional)
1/4 teaspoon salt

1. In large bowl with mixer at medium speed, beat peanut butter, margarine, brown sugar, corn syrup and eggs until smooth. Reduce speed; beat in 2 cups flour, baking powder, cinnamon and salt. With spoon, stir in remaining 2 cups flour. Wrap dough in plastic wrap; refrigerate 2 hours.

2. Preheat oven to 325°F. Divide dough in half; set aside half.

3. On floured surface roll out half the dough to 1/8-inch thickness. Cut with floured bear cookie cutter. Repeat with remaining dough.

4. Use scraps of dough to make bear faces. Make one small ball of dough for muzzle. Form 3 smaller balls of dough and press gently to create eyes and nose.

5. Bake bears on ungreased cookie sheets 10 minutes or until lightly browned. Remove from cookie sheets; cool completely on wire rack. Decorate as desired using frosting to create paws, ears and bow ties.

Makes about 3 dozen bears

Prep Time: 35 minutes plus chilling
Bake Time: 10 minutes plus cooling

Peanut Butter Bears

Apple Sauce Gingerbread Cookies

4 cups all-purpose flour

2 teaspoons ground ginger

2 teaspoons ground cinnamon

1 teaspoon baking soda

$1/2$ teaspoon salt

$1/4$ teaspoon ground nutmeg

$1/2$ cup butter, softened

1 cup sugar

$1/3$ cup GRANDMA'S® Molasses

1 cup MOTT'S® Natural Apple Sauce

Decorator Icing (recipe follows)

Heat oven to 350°F. In large bowl, sift together flour, ginger, cinnamon, baking soda, salt and nutmeg; set aside. In bowl of electric mixer, fitted with paddle, beat butter, sugar and molasses until creamy. Alternately blend in dry ingredients and apple sauce. Cover and chill dough for several hours or overnight.

On floured surface, roll dough out to $1/8$-inch thickness with lightly floured rolling pin. Cut with floured cookie cutter. Place on greased baking sheet. Bake 12 minutes or until done. Remove from sheet; cool on wire rack. Frost with Decorator Icing as desired. After icing dries, store in airtight container.   *Makes $2^1/2$ dozen ($5^1/2$-inch) cookies*

Decorator Icing: Mix 2 cups confectioners' sugar and 1 tablespoon water. Add more water, 1 teaspoon at a time, until icing holds its shape and can be piped through decorating tube.

Kringle's Cutouts

$^2/_3$ Butter Flavor CRISCO® Stick or $^2/_3$ cup Butter Flavor
   CRISCO® all-vegetable shortening
$^3/_4$ cup sugar
1 tablespoon plus 1 teaspoon milk
1 teaspoon vanilla
1 egg
2 cups all-purpose flour
$1^1/_2$ teaspoons baking powder
$^1/_4$ teaspoon salt

1. Cream shortening, sugar, milk and vanilla in large bowl at medium speed of electric mixer until well blended. Beat in egg. Combine flour, baking powder and salt. Mix into creamed mixture. Cover; refrigerate several hours or overnight.

2. Heat oven to 375°F. Place sheets of foil on countertop for cooling cookies.

3. Roll dough, half at a time, to $^1/_8$-inch thickness on floured surface. Cut into desired shapes. Place cookies 2 inches apart on ungreased cookie sheet. Sprinkle with colored sugar and decors, or leave plain to frost when cool.

4. Bake at 375°F for 7 to 9 minutes. *Do not overbake.* Cool 2 minutes on baking sheet. Remove cookies to foil to cool completely.

Makes about 3 dozen cookies

Hint: Floured pastry cloth and rolling pin cover make rolling out dough easier.

Orange-Almond Sables

1 1/2 cups powdered sugar

1 cup butter, softened

1 tablespoon finely grated orange peel

1 teaspoon almond extract

3/4 cup whole blanched almonds, toasted*

1 3/4 cups all-purpose flour

1/4 teaspoon salt

1 egg, beaten

To toast almonds, spread in single layer on baking sheet. Bake in preheated 350°F oven 8 to 10 minutes or until brown, stirring twice.

1. Preheat oven to 375°F.

2. Beat powdered sugar and butter in large bowl with electric mixer at medium speed until light and fluffy. Beat in orange peel and almond extract.

3. Set aside 24 whole almonds. Place remaining cooled almonds in food processor. Process using on/off pulsing action until almonds are ground, but not pasty.

4. Place ground almonds, flour and salt in medium bowl; stir to combine. Gradually add to butter mixture. Beat with electric mixer at low speed until well blended.

5. Place dough on lightly floured surface. Roll out dough with lightly floured rolling pin to just under 1/4-inch thickness. Cut dough with floured 2 1/2-inch fluted or round cookie cutter. Place dough 2 inches apart on ungreased cookie sheets.

6. Lightly brush tops of cookies with beaten egg. Press one whole reserved almond in center of each cookie. Brush almond lightly with beaten egg. Bake 10 to 12 minutes or until light golden brown.

7. Let cookies stand 1 minute on cookie sheets. Remove cookies with spatula to wire racks; cool completely. Store tightly covered at room temperature, or freeze up to 3 months.   *Makes about 2 dozen cookies*

Orange-Almond Sables

Christmas Cookie Pops

1 package (20 ounces) refrigerated sugar cookie dough
All-purpose flour (optional)
20 to 24 (4-inch) lollipop sticks
Royal Icing (recipe on page 11)
6 ounces almond bark (vanilla or chocolate) or butterscotch chips
Shortening
Assorted small candies

1. Preheat oven to 350°F. Grease cookie sheets; set aside. Remove dough from wrapper according to package directions.

2. Sprinkle dough with flour to minimize sticking, if necessary. Cut dough in half. Reserve 1 half; refrigerate remaining dough.

3. Roll reserved dough to $\frac{1}{3}$-inch thickness. Cut out cookies using $3\frac{1}{4}$- or $3\frac{1}{2}$-inch Christmas cookie cutters. Place lollipop sticks on cookies so that tips of sticks are imbedded in cookies. Carefully turn cookies with spatula so sticks are in back; place on prepared cookie sheets. Repeat with remaining dough.

4. Bake 7 to 11 minutes or until edges are lightly browned. Cool cookies on sheets 2 minutes. Remove cookies to wire racks; cool completely.

5. Prepare Royal Icing.

6. Melt almond bark in medium microwavable bowl according to package directions. Add 1 or more tablespoons shortening if coating is too thick. Hold cookies over bowl; spoon coating over cookies. Scrape excess coating from cookie edges. Decorate with small candies and Royal Icing immediately. Place cookies on wire racks set over waxed paper; let set. Store in tin at room temperature. *Makes 20 to 24 cookies*

Christmas Cookie Pops

Buttery Almond Cutouts

1 cup butter, softened
1 1/2 cups granulated sugar
3/4 cup sour cream
2 eggs
3 teaspoons almond extract, divided
1 teaspoon vanilla
4 1/3 cups all-purpose flour
1 teaspoon baking powder
1 teaspoon baking soda
1/2 teaspoon salt
2 cups powdered sugar
2 tablespoons milk
1 tablespoon light corn syrup
Assorted food colorings

1. Beat butter and granulated sugar in large bowl until light and fluffy. Add sour cream, eggs, 2 teaspoons almond extract and vanilla; beat until smooth. Add flour, baking powder, baking soda and salt; beat just until well blended.

2. Divide dough into 4 pieces; flatten each piece into a disc. Wrap each disc tightly with plastic wrap. Refrigerate at least 3 hours or up to 3 days.

3. Combine powdered sugar, milk, corn syrup and remaining 1 teaspoon almond extract in small bowl; stir until smooth. Cover and refrigerate up to 3 days.

4. Preheat oven to 375°F. Working with 1 disc of dough at a time, roll out on floured surface to 1/4-inch thickness. Cut dough into desired shapes using 2 1/2-inch cookie cutters. Place about 2 inches apart on ungreased

baking sheets. Bake 7 to 8 minutes or until edges are firm and bottoms are brown. Remove from baking sheets to wire racks to cool.

5. Separate powdered sugar mixture into 3 or 4 batches in small bowls; tint each batch with desired food coloring. Frost cookies.

Makes about 3 dozen cookies

Note: To freeze dough, place wrapped discs in resealable plastic food storage bags. Thaw at room temperature before using. Or, cut out dough, bake and cool cookies completely. Freeze unglazed cookies for up to 2 months. Thaw and glaze as desired.

Make-Ahead Time: refrigerate up to 3 days or freeze up to 3 months
Final Prep Time: 30 minutes

Buttery Almond Cutouts

Colorful Sugar Cutouts

$^1/_2$ cup (1 stick) butter or margarine

$^1/_4$ cup solid vegetable shortening

1 cup granulated sugar

2 large eggs

$^1/_2$ teaspoon vanilla extract

2$^3/_4$ cups all-purpose flour

$^1/_2$ teaspoon baking powder

$^1/_4$ teaspoon baking soda

$^1/_4$ teaspoon salt

Vanilla Icing (recipe follows)

"M&M's"® Chocolate Mini Baking Bits for decoration

In large bowl cream butter, shortening and sugar until light and fluffy; beat in eggs and vanilla. In medium bowl combine flour, baking powder, baking soda and salt; blend into creamed mixture. Wrap and refrigerate dough 2 to 3 hours. Preheat oven to 350°F. Working with half the dough at a time on lightly floured surface, roll to $^1/_8$-inch thickness. Cut into desired shapes using 3-inch cookie cutters. Using rigid spatula carefully transfer to ungreased cookie sheets. Bake 8 to 10 minutes. Cool completely on wire racks. Frost with Vanilla Icing and decorate with "M&M's"® Chocolate Mini Baking Bits. Store in tightly covered container.

Makes about 4 dozen cookies

Vanilla Icing: Beat 6 tablespoons butter and 4 cups powdered sugar until well blended; add $^1/_2$ teaspoon vanilla extract. Blend in 3 to 4 tablespoons milk, one tablespoon at a time, until of spreading consistency. Divide icing evenly into 3 small bowls. Add red food coloring to one and green to another until mixtures are of desired color. Leave the third portion white.

Peanut Butter Cut-Outs

$^1/_2$ cup SKIPPY® Creamy Peanut Butter

6 tablespoons margarine or butter, softened

$^1/_2$ cup packed brown sugar

$^1/_3$ cup KARO® Light or Dark Corn Syrup

1 egg

2 cups flour, divided

1 $^1/_2$ teaspoons baking powder

1 teaspoon ground cinnamon (optional)

$^1/_8$ teaspoon salt

1. In large bowl with mixer at medium speed, beat peanut butter, margarine, brown sugar, corn syrup and egg until smooth. Reduce speed; beat in 1 cup flour, baking powder, cinnamon and salt. With spoon, stir in remaining 1 cup flour.

2. Divide dough in half. Between two sheets of waxed paper on large cookie sheets, roll each half of dough $^1/_4$ inch thick. Refrigerate until firm, about 1 hour.

3. Preheat oven to 350°F. Remove top piece of waxed paper. With floured cookie cutters, cut dough into shapes. Place on ungreased cookie sheets.

4. Bake 10 minutes or until lightly browned. *Do not overbake.* Let stand on cookie sheets 2 minutes. Remove from cookie sheets; cool completely on wire racks. Reroll dough trimmings and cut additional cookies. Decorate as desired. *Makes about 5 dozen cookies*

Prep Time: 20 minutes, plus chilling and decorating
Bake Time: 10 minutes, plus cooling

Elves' Best Bar Cookies

Chocolate Espresso Brownies

The elves do more than just wrap presents. Those little guys also make sure Santa's well-stocked with delicious bar cookies for the long journey ahead.

Chocolate Espresso Brownies

4 squares (1 ounce each) unsweetened chocolate

1 cup sugar

1/4 cup Dried Plum Purée (recipe follows) or prepared dried plum
   butter

3 egg whites

1 to 2 tablespoons instant espresso coffee powder

1 teaspoon baking powder

1 teaspoon salt

1 teaspoon vanilla

1/2 cup all-purpose flour

Powdered sugar (optional)

Preheat oven to 350°F. Coat 8-inch square baking pan with vegetable cooking spray. In small heavy saucepan, melt chocolate over very low heat, stirring until melted and smooth. Remove from heat; cool. In mixer bowl, beat chocolate and remaining ingredients except flour and powdered sugar at medium speed until well blended; mix in flour. Spread batter evenly in prepared pan. Bake in center of oven about 30 minutes until pick inserted into center comes out clean. Cool completely in pan on wire rack. Dust with powdered sugar. Cut into 1 1/3-inch squares.   *Makes 36 brownies*

Dried Plum Purée: Combine 1 1/3 cups (8 ounces) pitted dried plums and 6 tablespoons hot water in container of food processor or blender. Pulse on and off until dried plums are finely chopped and smooth. Store leftovers in a covered container in the refrigerator for up to two months. Makes 1 cup.

Favorite recipe from **California Dried Plum Board**

Rocky Road Bars

2 cups (12-ounce package) NESTLÉ® TOLL HOUSE® Semi-
    Sweet Chocolate Morsels, divided
1 1/2 cups all-purpose flour
1 1/2 teaspoons baking powder
1 cup granulated sugar
6 tablespoons (3/4 stick) butter or margarine, softened
1 1/2 teaspoons vanilla extract
2 eggs
2 cups (4 ounces) miniature marshmallows
1 1/2 cups coarsely chopped walnuts

MICROWAVE 1 cup morsels in medium, microwave-safe bowl on
HIGH (100% power) for 1 minute; stir. Microwave at additional 10- to
20-second intervals; stir until smooth. Cool to room temperature.
Combine flour and baking powder in small bowl.

BEAT sugar, butter and vanilla in large mixer bowl until crumbly. Beat in
eggs. Add melted chocolate; beat until smooth. Gradually beat in flour
mixture. Spread batter into greased 13×9-inch baking pan.

BAKE in preheated 375°F. oven for 16 to 20 minutes or until wooden
pick inserted in center comes out still slightly sticky.

REMOVE from oven; sprinkle immediately with marshmallows, nuts and
remaining 1 cup morsels. Return to oven for 2 minutes. Remove from
oven; cool in pan on wire rack.   *Makes 2 1/2 dozen bars*

Rocky Road Bars

Chocolate Cheese Ripple Bars

CHEESE BATTER

   2 (3-ounce) packages cream cheese, softened

   2 eggs

   $^1/_4$ cup sugar

   2 tablespoons all-purpose flour

   2 tablespoons ($^1/_4$ stick) butter, softened

CHOCOLATE BATTER

   1 cup all-purpose flour

   1 cup sugar

   $^3/_4$ teaspoon baking soda

   $^3/_4$ teaspoon salt

   $^1/_2$ cup milk

   $^1/_3$ cup ($5^1/_3$ tablespoons) butter, softened

   $1^1/_4$ teaspoons vinegar

   3 envelopes (3 ounces) NESTLÉ® Choco Bake® Unsweetened
      Baking Chocolate Flavor

   2 eggs

   $1^1/_4$ teaspoons vanilla extract

For cheese batter

Preheat oven to 350°F. In small mixer bowl beat cream cheese, eggs, sugar, flour and butter until creamy; set aside.

For chocolate batter

In large mixer bowl, combine flour, sugar, baking soda and salt. Beat in milk, butter, vinegar and unsweetened baking chocolate flavor. Blend in eggs and vanilla extract until smooth. Pour into greased 13×9×2-inch baking pan. Spoon cheese batter over top. Swirl knife through batters to ripple slightly.

Bake 25 to 30 minutes. Cool completely in pan on wire rack; cut into 2-inch squares.   *Makes 2 dozen squares*

Chocolate Chip Cranberry Cheese Bars

        1 cup (2 sticks) butter or margarine, softened
        1 cup packed brown sugar
        2 cups all-purpose flour
    1½ cups quick or old-fashioned oats
        2 teaspoons grated orange peel
        2 cups (12-ounce package) NESTLÉ® TOLL HOUSE® Semi-Sweet
            Chocolate Morsels
        1 cup (4 ounces) dried cranberries
        1 package (8 ounces) cream cheese, softened
    1¼ cups (14-ounce can) CARNATION® Sweetened Condensed Milk

BEAT butter and brown sugar in large mixer bowl until creamy. Gradually beat in flour, oats and orange peel until crumbly. Stir in morsels and cranberries; reserve 2 cups mixture. Press remaining mixture onto bottom of greased 13×9-inch baking pan.

BAKE in preheated 350°F. oven for 15 minutes. Beat cream cheese in small mixer bowl until smooth. Gradually beat in sweetened condensed milk. Pour over hot crust; sprinkle with reserved flour mixture. Bake for additional 25 to 30 minutes or until center is set. Cool in pan on wire rack.
                                      Makes about 3 dozen bars

Festive Fruited White Chip Blondies

¹/₂ cup (1 stick) butter or margarine

1²/₃ cups (10-ounce package) HERSHEY'S Premier White Chips, divided

2 eggs

¹/₄ cup granulated sugar

1¹/₄ cups all-purpose flour

¹/₃ cup orange juice

³/₄ cup cranberries, chopped

¹/₄ cup chopped dried apricots

¹/₂ cup coarsely chopped nuts

¹/₄ cup packed light brown sugar

1. Heat oven to 325°F. Grease and flour 9-inch square baking pan.

2. Melt butter in medium saucepan; stir in 1 cup white chips. In large bowl, beat eggs until foamy. Add granulated sugar; beat until thick and pale yellow in color. Add flour, orange juice and white chip mixture; beat just until combined. Spread one-half of batter, about 1¹/₄ cups, into prepared pan.

3. Bake 15 minutes or until edges are lightly browned; remove from oven.

4. Stir cranberries, apricots and remaining ²/₃ cup white chips into remaining one-half of batter; spread over top of hot baked mixture. Stir together nuts and brown sugar; sprinkle over top.

5. Bake 25 to 30 minutes or until edges are lightly browned. Cool completely in pan on wire rack. Cut into bars.   *Makes about 16 bars*

Festive Fruited White Chip Blondies

Oatmeal Brownie Gems

2¾ cups quick-cooking or old-fashioned oats, uncooked

1 cup all-purpose flour

1 cup firmly packed light brown sugar

1 cup coarsely chopped walnuts

1 teaspoon baking soda

1 cup butter or margarine, melted

1¾ cups "M&M's"® Semi-Sweet Chocolate Mini Baking Bits

1 (19- to 21-ounce) package fudge brownie mix, prepared
according to package directions for fudge-like brownies

Preheat oven to 350°F. In large bowl combine oats, flour, sugar, nuts and baking soda; add butter until mixture forms coarse crumbs. Toss in "M&M's"® Semi-Sweet Chocolate Mini Baking Bits until evenly distributed. Reserve 3 cups mixture. Pat remaining mixture onto bottom of 15×10×1-inch pan to form crust. Pour prepared brownie mix over crust, carefully spreading into thin layer. Sprinkle reserved crumb mixture over top of brownie mixture; pat down lightly. Bake 25 to 30 minutes or until toothpick inserted in center comes out with moist crumbs. Cool completely. Cut into bars. Store in tightly covered container.

Makes 48 bars

Oatmeal Brownie Gems

Lemon Bars

CRUST

    1 cup all-purpose flour

    $1/2$ cup powdered sugar

    $1/4$ cup MOTT'S® Natural Apple Sauce

    2 tablespoons margarine, melted

LEMON FILLING

    1 cup granulated sugar

    2 egg whites

    1 whole egg

    $1/3$ cup MOTT'S® Natural Apple Sauce

    1 teaspoon grated lemon peel

    $1/4$ cup lemon juice

    3 tablespoons all-purpose flour

    $1/2$ teaspoon baking powder

    Additional powdered sugar (optional)

1. Preheat oven to 350°F. Spray 8-inch square baking pan with nonstick cooking spray.

2. To prepare crust, in small bowl, combine 1 cup flour and powdered sugar. Add $1/4$ cup apple sauce and margarine. Stir with fork until mixture resembles coarse crumbs. Press evenly into bottom of prepared pan. Bake 10 minutes.

3. To prepare lemon filling, in medium bowl, beat granulated sugar, egg whites and whole egg with electric mixer at medium speed until thick and smooth. Add $1/3$ cup apple sauce, lemon peel, lemon juice, 3 tablespoons flour and baking powder. Beat until well blended. Pour lemon filling over baked crust.

4. Bake 20 to 25 minutes or until lightly browned. Cool completely on wire rack. Sprinkle with additional powdered sugar, if desired; cut into 14 bars.   *Makes 14 servings*

Double-Decker Cereal Treats

   1 2/3 cups (10-ounce package) REESE'S® Peanut Butter Chips
   2 tablespoons vegetable oil
   2 teaspoons vanilla extract, divided
   2 cups (12-ounce package) HERSHEY'S Semi-Sweet Chocolate
      Chips
   2 cups light corn syrup
1 1/3 cups packed light brown sugar
  12 cups crisp rice cereal, divided

1. Line 15 1/2 × 10 1/2 × 1-inch jelly-roll pan with foil, extending foil over edges of pan.

2. Place peanut butter chips, oil and 1 teaspoon vanilla in large bowl. Place chocolate chips and remaining 1 teaspoon vanilla in second large bowl. Stir together corn syrup and brown sugar in large saucepan; cook over medium heat, stirring constantly, until mixture comes to full rolling boil. Remove from heat. Immediately pour half of hot mixture into each reserved bowl; stir each mixture until chips are melted and mixture is smooth. Immediately stir 6 cups rice cereal into each of the two mixtures. Spread peanut butter mixture into prepared pan; spread chocolate mixture over top of peanut butter layer.

3. Cool completely. Use foil to lift treats out of pan; peel off foil. Cut treats into bars. Store in tightly covered container in cool, dry place.

Makes about 6 dozen pieces

Oatmeal Toffee Bars

1 cup (2 sticks) butter or margarine, softened

$^1/_2$ cup packed light brown sugar

$^1/_2$ cup granulated sugar

2 eggs

1 teaspoon vanilla extract

$1^1/_2$ cups all-purpose flour

1 teaspoon baking soda

$^1/_2$ teaspoon ground cinnamon

$^1/_2$ teaspoon salt

3 cups quick-cooking or regular rolled oats

$1^3/_4$ cups (10-ounce package) SKOR® English Toffee Bits *or*
    $1^3/_4$ cups HEATH® BITS 'O BRICKLE™, divided

1. Heat oven to 350°F. Grease 13×9×2-inch baking pan.

2. Beat butter, brown sugar and granulated sugar in large bowl until well blended. Add eggs and vanilla; beat well. Stir together flour, baking soda, cinnamon and salt; gradually add to butter mixture, beating until well blended. Stir in oats and $1^1/_3$ cups toffee bits (mixture will be stiff). Spread mixture into prepared pan.

3. Bake 25 minutes or until wooden pick inserted in center comes out clean. Immediately sprinkle remaining toffee bits over surface. Cool completely in pan on wire rack. Cut into bars.   *Makes about 36 bars*

Tip: Bar cookies can be cut into different shapes for variety. To cut into triangles, cut cookie bars into 2- to 3-inch squares, then diagonally cut each square in half. To make diamond shapes, cut parallel lines 2 inches apart across the length of the pan, then cut diagonal lines 2 inches apart.

Oatmeal Toffee Bars

Cinnamony Apple Streusel Bars

1¼ cups graham cracker crumbs

1¼ cups all-purpose flour

¾ cup packed brown sugar, divided

¼ cup granulated sugar

1 teaspoon ground cinnamon

¾ cup butter, melted

2 cups chopped apples (2 medium apples, cored and peeled)

Glaze (recipe follows)

Preheat oven to 350°F. Grease 13×9-inch baking pan. Combine graham cracker crumbs, flour, ½ cup brown sugar, granulated sugar, cinnamon and melted butter in large bowl until well blended; reserve 1 cup. Press remaining crumb mixture into bottom of prepared pan. Bake 8 minutes. Remove from oven; set aside.

Toss remaining ¼ cup brown sugar with apples in medium bowl until dissolved; arrange apples over baked crust. Sprinkle reserved 1 cup crumb mixture over filling. Bake 30 to 35 minutes or until apples are tender. Remove pan to wire rack; cool completely. Drizzle with Glaze. Cut into bars. *Makes 3 dozen bars*

Glaze: Combine ½ cup powdered sugar and 1 tablespoon milk in small bowl until well blended.

Cinnamony Apple Streusel Bars

Divine Double Dark Brownies

¹/₂ cup KARO® Light or Dark Corn Syrup

¹/₂ cup (1 stick) margarine or butter

5 squares (1 ounce each) semisweet chocolate

³/₄ cup sugar

3 eggs

1 cup all-purpose flour

1 cup chopped walnuts

1 teaspoon vanilla

Chocolate Glaze (recipe follows)

1. Preheat oven to 350°F. Grease and flour one 9-inch round cake pan.

2. In large saucepan over medium heat, bring corn syrup and margarine to a boil, stirring occasionally; remove from heat. Add chocolate; stir until melted. Add sugar; stir in eggs, one at a time, until blended. Add flour, nuts and vanilla. Pour into prepared pan.

3. Bake 30 minutes or until wooden pick inserted in center comes out clean. Cool in pan 10 minutes. Remove from pan; cool on wire rack.

4. Prepare Chocolate Glaze; pour over top and spread on side. Let stand 1 hour. *Makes 8 servings*

Chocolate Glaze: In small saucepan over low heat, melt 3 squares (1 ounce each) semisweet chocolate and 1 tablespoon margarine or butter, stirring often. Remove from heat. Stir in 2 tablespoons KARO® Light or Dark Corn Syrup and 1 teaspoon milk until smooth.

Prep Time: 15 minutes
Bake Time: 30 minutes, plus cooling

Chocolate Pecan Pie Bars

CRUST

$1^{1}/_{2}$ cups all-purpose flour

$^{1}/_{2}$ cup (1 stick) butter, softened

$^{1}/_{4}$ cup firmly packed brown sugar

FILLING

3 eggs

$^{3}/_{4}$ cup dark or light corn syrup

$^{3}/_{4}$ cup granulated sugar

2 tablespoons ($^{1}/_{4}$ stick) butter, melted

1 teaspoon vanilla extract

$1^{1}/_{2}$ cups coarsely chopped pecans

2 cups (12-ounce package) NESTLÉ® TOLL HOUSE® Semi-Sweet Chocolate Morsels

For Crust

BEAT flour, butter and brown sugar in small mixer bowl until crumbly. Press into greased 13×9-inch baking pan. Bake in preheated 350°F. oven for 12 to 15 minutes until lightly browned.

For Filling

BEAT eggs, corn syrup, granulated sugar, melted butter and vanilla in medium bowl with wire whisk. Stir in pecans and morsels. Pour evenly over baked crust. Bake in preheated 350°F. oven for 25 to 30 minutes until set. Cool.   *Makes about 3 dozen bars*

Triple Layer Peanut Butter Bars

BASE

1¼ cups firmly packed light brown sugar

¾ cup creamy peanut butter

½ CRISCO® Stick or ½ cup CRISCO® all-vegetable shortening
plus additional for greasing

3 tablespoons milk

1 tablespoon vanilla

1 egg

1¾ cups all-purpose flour

¾ teaspoon baking soda

¾ teaspoon salt

PEANUT BUTTER LAYER

1½ cups confectioners' sugar

2 tablespoons creamy peanut butter

1 tablespoon Butter Flavor CRISCO® Stick or 1 tablespoon
Butter Flavor CRISCO® all-vegetable shortening

3 tablespoons milk

CHOCOLATE GLAZE

2 squares (1 ounce each) unsweetened baking chocolate

2 tablespoons Butter Flavor CRISCO® Stick or 2 tablespoons
Butter Flavor CRISCO® all-vegetable shortening

1. Heat oven to 350°F. Grease 13×9-inch baking pan. Place cooling rack on counter top.

2. For base, place brown sugar, peanut butter, shortening, milk and vanilla in a large bowl. Beat at medium speed of electric mixer until well blended. Add egg; beat until just blended.

3. Combine flour, baking soda and salt. Add to shortening mixture; beat at low speed just until blended.

4. Press mixture evenly onto bottom of prepared pan.

5. Bake at 350°F for 18 to 20 minutes or unitl wooden pick inserted in center comes out clean. *Do not overbake.* Cool completely on cooling rack.

6. For peanut butter layer, place confectioners' sugar, peanut butter, shortening and milk in medium bowl. Beat at low speed of electric mixer until smooth. Spread over base. Refrigerate 30 minutes.

7. For chocolate glaze, place chocolate and shortening in small microwave-safe bowl. Microwave at 50% (MEDIUM) for 1 to 2 minutes or until shiny and soft. Stir until smooth. Cool slightly. Spread over peanut butter layer. Refrigerate about 1 hour or until glaze is set. Cut into $3 \times 1^{1}/_{2}$-inch bars. Let stand 15 to 20 minutes at room temperature before serving. *Makes about 2 dozen bars*

Triple Layer Peanut Butter Bars

Mrs. Claus's Treasures

Original Nestlé® Toll House® Chocolate Chip Cookies

Looking for the quintessential holiday drop cookies? Here are a few straight from the first lady of Christmas, any of which would be perfect to leave out for Santa on the big night!

Original Nestlé® Toll House® Chocolate Chip Cookies

2¼ cups all-purpose flour

1 teaspoon baking soda

1 teaspoon salt

1 cup (2 sticks) butter, softened

¾ cup granulated sugar

¾ cup packed brown sugar

1 teaspoon vanilla extract

2 eggs

2 cups (12-ounce package) NESTLÉ® TOLL HOUSE® Semi-Sweet Chocolate Morsels

1 cup chopped nuts

COMBINE flour, baking soda and salt in small bowl. Beat butter, granulated sugar, brown sugar and vanilla in large mixer bowl. Add eggs, one at a time, beating well after each addition. Gradually beat in flour mixture. Stir in morsels and nuts. Drop by rounded tablespoon onto ungreased baking sheets.

BAKE in preheated 375°F. oven for 9 to 11 minutes or until golden brown. Cool on baking sheets for 2 minutes; remove to wire racks to cool completely. *Makes about 5 dozen cookies*

Pan Cookie Variation: PREPARE dough as above. Spread into greased 15½×10½-inch jelly-roll pan. Bake in preheated 375°F. oven for 20 to 25 minutes or until golden brown. Cool in pan on wire rack.

Makes 4 dozen bars

Sour Cream Chocolate Chip Cookies

1 Butter Flavor CRISCO® Stick or 1 cup Butter Flavor
   CRISCO® all-vegetable shortening plus additional for
   greasing
1 cup firmly packed brown sugar
$^{1}/_{2}$ cup granulated sugar
1 egg
$^{1}/_{2}$ cup dairy sour cream
$^{1}/_{4}$ cup warm honey
2 teaspoons vanilla
$2^{1}/_{2}$ cups all-purpose flour
$1^{1}/_{2}$ teaspoons baking powder
$^{1}/_{2}$ teaspoon salt
2 cups semi-sweet or milk chocolate chips
1 cup coarsely chopped walnuts

1. Heat oven to 375°F. Grease cookie sheet. Place sheets of foil on countertop for cooling cookies.

2. Combine 1 cup shortening, brown sugar and granulated sugar in large bowl. Beat at medium speed of electric mixer until well blended. Beat in egg, sour cream, honey and vanilla. Beat until just blended.

3. Combine flour, baking powder and salt. Mix into creamed mixture at low speed until just blended. Stir in chocolate chips and nuts.

4. Drop slightly rounded measuring tablespoonfuls of dough 2 inches apart onto prepared cookie sheet.

5. Bake at 375°F 10 to 12 minutes or until set. *Do not overbake.* Cool 2 minutes on baking sheet. Remove to foil to cool completely.

Makes about 5 dozen cookies

Sour Cream Chocolate Chip Cookies

Gingersnaps

2½ cups all-purpose flour

1½ teaspoons ground ginger

1 teaspoon baking soda

1 teaspoon ground allspice

½ teaspoon salt

1½ cups sugar

2 tablespoons margarine, softened

½ cup MOTT'S® Apple Sauce

¼ cup GRANDMA'S® Molasses

1. Preheat oven to 375°F. Spray cookie sheet with nonstick cooking spray.

2. In medium bowl, sift together flour, ginger, baking soda, allspice and salt.

3. In large bowl, beat sugar and margarine with electric mixer at medium speed until blended. Whisk in apple sauce and molasses.

4. Add flour mixture to apple sauce mixture; stir until well blended.

5. Drop rounded tablespoonfuls of dough 1 inch apart onto prepared cookie sheet. Flatten each slightly with moistened fingertips.

6. Bake 12 to 15 minutes or until firm. Cool completely on wire rack.

Makes 3 dozen cookies

Gingersnaps and Oatmeal Cookies (page 60)

Chunky Butter Christmas Cookies

1¼ cups butter, softened

1 cup packed brown sugar

½ cup dairy sour cream

1 egg

2 teaspoons vanilla

1½ cups all-purpose flour

1 teaspoon baking soda

1 teaspoon salt

1½ cups old-fashioned or quick oats, uncooked

1 (10-ounce) package white chocolate pieces

1 cup flaked coconut

1 (3½-ounce) jar macadamia nuts, coarsely chopped

Beat butter and sugar in large bowl until light and fluffy. Blend in sour cream, egg and vanilla. Add combined flour, baking soda and salt; mix well. Stir in oats, white chocolate pieces, coconut and nuts. Drop rounded teaspoonfuls of dough, 2 inches apart, onto ungreased cookie sheet. Bake in preheated 375°F oven 10 to 12 minutes or until edges are lightly browned. Cool 1 minute; remove to cooling rack.

Makes 5 dozen cookies

Favorite recipe from **Wisconsin Milk Marketing Board**

54

Holiday Fruit Drops

$^1/_2$ cup butter, softened

$^3/_4$ cup packed brown sugar

1 egg

1 $^1/_4$ cups all-purpose flour

1 teaspoon vanilla

$^1/_2$ teaspoon baking soda

$^1/_2$ teaspoon ground cinnamon

Pinch salt

1 cup (8 ounces) diced candied pineapple

1 cup (8 ounces) whole red and green candied cherries*

8 ounces chopped pitted dates

1 cup (6 ounces) semisweet chocolate chips

$^1/_2$ cup whole hazelnuts*

$^1/_2$ cup pecan halves*

$^1/_2$ cup coarsely chopped walnuts

*The cherries, hazelnuts and pecan halves are not chopped, but left whole.

Preheat oven to 325°F. Lightly grease cookie sheets or line with parchment paper. Cream butter and brown sugar in large bowl. Beat in egg until light and fluffy. Mix in flour, vanilla, baking soda, cinnamon and salt. Stir in pineapple, cherries, dates, chocolate chips, hazelnuts, pecans and walnuts. Drop dough by rounded teaspoonfuls 2 inches apart onto prepared cookie sheets.

Bake 15 to 20 minutes or until firm and lightly browned around edges. Remove to wire racks to cool completely.   *Makes about 8 dozen cookies*

Cocoa Hazelnut Macaroons

$^1/_3$ cup hazelnuts

$^3/_4$ cup quick oats

$^1/_3$ cup brown sugar

6 tablespoons unsweetened cocoa powder

2 tablespoons all-purpose flour

4 egg whites

1 teaspoon vanilla

$^1/_2$ teaspoon salt

$^1/_3$ cup plus 1 tablespoon granulated sugar

1. Preheat oven to 375°F. Bake hazelnuts 8 minutes or until lightly browned. Quickly transfer nuts to clean dry dish towel. Fold towel; rub vigorously to remove as much of the skins as possible. Finely chop using food processor, nut grinder or chef's knife. Combine with oats, brown sugar, cocoa and flour in medium bowl; mix well. Set aside.

2. *Reduce oven temperature to 325°F.* Combine egg whites, vanilla and salt in clean dry medium mixing bowl. Beat with electric mixer on high until soft peaks form. Gradually add granulated sugar, continuing to beat on high until stiff peaks form. Gently fold in hazelnut mixture with rubber spatula.

3. Drop level measuring tablespoonfuls onto cookie sheet. Bake 15 to 17 minutes or until tops of cookies no longer appear wet. Transfer to cooling rack. Store in loosely covered container.

Makes 3 dozen cookies (3 cookies per serving)

Cocoa Hazelnut Macaroons

Oatmeal Scotchies™

1 1/4 cups all-purpose flour

1 teaspoon baking soda

1/2 teaspoon salt

1/2 teaspoon ground cinnamon

1 cup (2 sticks) butter or margarine, softened

3/4 cup granulated sugar

3/4 cup packed brown sugar

2 eggs

1 teaspoon vanilla extract *or* grated peel of 1 orange

3 cups quick or old-fashioned oats

1 2/3 cups (11-ounce package) NESTLÉ® TOLL HOUSE®
    Butterscotch Flavored Morsels

COMBINE flour, baking soda, salt and cinnamon in small bowl. Beat butter, granulated sugar, brown sugar, eggs and vanilla in large mixer bowl. Gradually beat in flour mixture. Stir in oats and morsels. Drop by rounded tablespoon onto ungreased baking sheets.

BAKE in preheated 375°F. oven for 7 to 8 minutes for chewy cookies; 9 to 10 minutes for crisp cookies. Cool on baking sheets for 2 minutes; remove to wire racks to cool completely.   *Makes about 4 dozen cookies*

Oatmeal Scotchie™ Pan Cookies: SPREAD dough into greased 15 1/2 × 10 1/2-inch jelly-roll pan. Bake in preheated 375°F. oven for 18 to 22 minutes or until very lightly browned. Cool completely on wire rack. Makes 4 dozen bars.

Oatmeal Scotchies™

Oatmeal Cookies

1 cup all-purpose flour

1 teaspoon baking powder

$^1/_2$ teaspoon baking soda

$^1/_2$ teaspoon salt

$^1/_2$ cup granulated sugar

$^1/_2$ cup firmly packed light brown sugar

$^1/_4$ cup MOTT'S® Cinnamon Apple Sauce

2 tablespoons vegetable shortening

1 egg *or* $^1/_4$ cup egg substitute

1 teaspoon vanilla extract

1$^1/_3$ cups uncooked rolled oats

$^1/_2$ cup raisins (optional)

Heat oven to 375°F. Lightly spray cookie sheet with cooking spray. In large bowl, mix flour, baking powder, baking soda and salt. In separate bowl, whisk together granulated and brown sugars, apple sauce, shortening, egg, and vanilla until shortening breaks into pea sized pieces. Add flour mixture to apple sauce mixture. Mix well. Fold in oats and raisins. Drop rounded teaspoonfuls onto cookie sheet; bake 5 minutes. Remove cookies from cookie sheet and cool completely on wire rack.

Makes 36 cookies

Coffee Chip Drops

1¼ cups firmly packed light brown sugar
¾ Butter Flavor CRISCO® Stick or ¾ cup Butter Flavor
    CRISCO® all-vegetable shortening
2 tablespoons cold coffee
1 teaspoon vanilla
1 egg
1¾ cups all-purpose flour
1 tablespoon finely ground French roast or espresso coffee beans
1 teaspoon salt
¾ teaspoon baking soda
½ cup semisweet chocolate chips
½ cup milk chocolate chips
½ cup coarsely chopped walnuts
30 to 40 chocolate kiss candies, unwrapped

1. Heat oven to 375°F. Place sheets of foil on countertop for cooling cookies.

2. Place brown sugar, shortening, coffee and vanilla in large bowl. Beat at medium speed of electric mixer until well blended. Add egg; beat well.

3. Combine flour, ground coffee, salt and baking soda. Add to shortening mixture; beat at low speed just until blended. Stir in chips and walnuts.

4. Drop dough by rounded measuring tablespoonfuls 2 inches apart onto ungreased baking sheets.

5. Bake one baking sheet at a time at 375°F for 8 to 10 minutes or until cookies are lightly browned and just set. *Do not overbake.* Place 1 candy in center of each cookie. Cool 2 minutes on baking sheet. Remove cookies to foil to cool completely. *Makes about 3 dozen cookies*

Sunny Cocoa Drop Cookies

$^1/_2$ cup (1 stick) 60% vegetable oil spread

$^2/_3$ cup granulated sugar

$^2/_3$ cup lowfat sour cream

1 egg white

1 teaspoon vanilla extract

$^1/_4$ teaspoon freshly grated orange peel

1$^3/_4$ cups all-purpose flour

3 tablespoons HERSHEY'S Cocoa

1 teaspoon baking soda

$^1/_2$ teaspoon baking powder

$^1/_4$ teaspoon ground cinnamon

Cocoa Glaze (recipe follows)

1. Heat oven to 350°F. Spray cookie sheet with vegetable cooking spray.

2. Beat vegetable oil spread and granulated sugar in large bowl on medium speed of mixer until fluffy. Add sour cream, egg white, vanilla and orange peel; beat until well blended. Stir together flour, cocoa, baking soda, baking powder and cinnamon; gradually add to sugar mixture, beating until blended. Drop dough by rounded teaspoons onto prepared cookie sheet.

3. Bake 10 to 12 minutes or until set. Remove from cookie sheet to wire rack. Cool completely. Prepare Cocoa Glaze; drizzle over tops of cookies. Store, covered, at room temperature.   *Makes 4 dozen cookies*

Prep Time: 30 minutes

Bake Time: 10 minutes

Cocoa Glaze

1 tablespoon 60% vegetable oil spread

2 tablespoons water

1 tablespoon HERSHEY'S® Cocoa

$^1/_2$ cup powdered sugar

$^1/_2$ teaspoon vanilla extract

Melt vegetable oil spread in small saucepan over low heat. Stir in water and cocoa. Cook, stirring constantly, until thick. *Do not boil.* Remove from heat; gradually add powdered sugar and vanilla, beating with spoon or whisk to drizzling consistency.   *Makes about $^1/_3$ cup glaze*

Sunny Cocoa Drop Cookies

Super Chunk Oatmeal Cookie Mix

1 cup sugar

1 teaspoon cinnamon

1 cup flour

$^1/_2$ teaspoon baking soda

$^1/_4$ teaspoon salt

1 cup quick-cooking rolled oats

1 package (12 ounces) BAKER'S® Semi-Sweet Chocolate Chunks, divided

$^1/_2$ cup chopped nuts

LAYER ingredients in $1^1/_2$-quart glass canister or jar in the following order: sugar mixed with cinnamon, flour, baking soda, salt, oats, chocolate chunks and nuts. Tap jar gently on counter to settle each layer before adding next one. Cover.

ATTACH baking directions (see below) to jar.   *Makes 1 gift jar*

BAKING DIRECTIONS

HEAT oven to 375°F. Beat $^3/_4$ cup ($1^1/_2$ sticks) softened butter, 1 egg and 1 teaspoon vanilla in large bowl with electric mixer on medium speed until well blended. Empty contents of jar into bowl. Stir until well mixed. Drop by heaping tablespoonfuls onto *ungreased* cookie sheets.

BAKE 12 to 13 minutes or until golden brown. Cool on cookie sheets 1 minute. Remove to wire racks and cool completely. Makes about 3 dozen cookies.

Super Chunk Oatmeal Cookie Mix

Santa's Favorite Shapes

Festive Fudge Blossoms

From crescents to pirouettes to logs, these super shaped cookies keep Santa going strong and in tip-top shape.

Festive Fudge Blossoms

$^{1}/_{4}$ cup butter, softened

1 box (18.25 ounces) chocolate fudge cake mix

1 egg, slightly beaten

2 tablespoons water

$^{3}/_{4}$ to 1 cup finely chopped walnuts

48 chocolate star candies

1. Preheat oven to 350°F. Cut butter into cake mix in large bowl until mixture resembles coarse crumbs. Stir in egg and water until well blended.

2. Shape dough into $^{1}/_{2}$-inch balls; roll in walnuts, pressing nuts gently into dough. Place about 2 inches apart on ungreased baking sheets.

3. Bake cookies 12 minutes or until puffed and nearly set. Place chocolate star in center of each cookie; bake 1 minute. Cool 2 minutes on baking sheets. Remove cookies from baking sheets to wire racks to cool completely. *Makes 4 dozen cookies*

Prep and Bake Time: 30 minutes

Banana Sandies

$2^{1}/_{3}$ cups all-purpose flour

1 cup butter, softened

$^{3}/_{4}$ cup granulated sugar

$^{1}/_{4}$ cup brown sugar

$^{1}/_{2}$ cup $^{1}/_{4}$-inch slices banana (about 1 medium)

1 teaspoon vanilla

$^{1}/_{4}$ teaspoon salt

$^{2}/_{3}$ cup chopped pecans

Prepared cream cheese frosting

Yellow food coloring (optional)

1. Preheat oven to 350°F. Combine flour, butter, sugars, banana slices, vanilla and salt in large bowl. Beat 2 to 3 minutes, scraping bowl often, until well blended. Stir in pecans. Shape rounded teaspoonfuls of dough into 1-inch balls. Place 2 inches apart on greased cookie sheets. Flatten cookies to $^{1}/_{4}$-inch thickness with bottom of glass dipped in sugar. Bake 12 to 15 minutes or until edges are lightly browned. Remove immediately to wire racks; cool completely.

2. Tint frosting with food coloring, if desired. Spread 1 tablespoon frosting over bottoms of $^{1}/_{2}$ the cookies. Top with remaining cookies.

Makes about 2 dozen sandwich cookies

Banana Sandies

Christmas Spritz Cookies

2 1/4 cups all-purpose flour

1/4 teaspoon salt

1 1/4 cups powdered sugar

1 cup butter, softened

1 egg

1 teaspoon almond extract

1 teaspoon vanilla

Green food coloring (optional)

Candied red and green cherries and assorted decorative candies (optional)

Icing (recipe follows, optional)

Preheat oven to 375°F. Place flour and salt in medium bowl; stir to combine. Beat powdered sugar and butter in large bowl until light and fluffy. Beat in egg, almond extract and vanilla. Gradually add flour mixture. Beat until well blended.

Divide dough in half. If desired, tint half of dough with green food coloring. Fit cookie press with desired plate (or change plates for different shapes after first batch). Fill press with dough; press dough 1 inch apart onto ungreased cookie sheets. Decorate cookies with cherries and assorted candies, if desired.

Bake 10 to 12 minutes or until just set. Remove cookies to wire racks; cool completely.

Prepare Icing, if desired. Pipe or drizzle on cooled cookies. Decorate with cherries and assorted candies, if desired. Store tightly covered at room temperature or freeze up to 3 months. *Makes about 5 dozen cookies*

Icing

    $1^{1}/_{2}$ cups powdered sugar
     2 tablespoons milk plus additional, if needed
    $^{1}/_{8}$ teaspoon almond extract

Place all ingredients in medium bowl; stir until thick, but spreadable. (If icing is too thick, stir in 1 teaspoon additional milk.)

Christmas Spritz Cookies

Chocolate-Flecked Pirouettes

$^1/_2$ cup butter, softened

$^1/_2$ cup sugar

2 egg whites

1 teaspoon vanilla

$^1/_2$ cup all-purpose flour

$^1/_3$ cup coarsely grated bittersweet or dark sweet chocolate bar
(about 2 ounces)

1. Preheat oven to 400°F. Grease cookie sheets well; set aside.

2. Beat butter and sugar in small bowl with electric mixer at medium speed until light and fluffy. Beat in egg whites, 1 at a time. Beat in vanilla. Add flour; beat at low speed just until blended. Gently fold in grated chocolate with rubber spatula.

3. Drop teaspoonfuls of batter 4 inches apart onto prepared cookie sheets. Spread dough into 2-inch rounds with small spatula. Make only 3 to 4 rounds per sheet.

4. Bake 1 sheet at a time 4 to 5 minutes until edges are barely golden. *Do not overbake.*

5. Remove from oven and quickly loosen edge of 1 cookie from baking sheet with thin spatula. Quickly roll cookie around clean handle of wooden spoon overlapping edges to form cigar shape. Repeat with remaining cookies. (If cookies become too firm to shape, return to oven for a few seconds to soften.) Slide cookie off handle to wire rack; cool completely.

6. Store tightly covered at room temperature or freeze up to 3 months.

Makes about 3 dozen cookies

Chocolate-Flecked Pirouettes

Holiday Sugar Cookies

2 cups all-purpose flour
$1/2$ teaspoon baking soda
1 cup FLEISCHMANN'S® Original Margarine, softened
1 cup plus 2 tablespoons sugar, divided
1 teaspoon vanilla extract
$1/4$ cup EGG BEATERS® Healthy Real Egg Product

1. Mix flour and baking soda in small bowl; set aside.

2. Beat margarine, 1 cup sugar and vanilla in large bowl with mixer at medium speed until creamy. Beat in Egg Beaters® until light and fluffy. Gradually blend in flour mixture. Wrap dough; refrigerate 4 hours.

3. Shape rounded teaspoons of dough into balls using floured hands. Place 2 inches apart on ungreased baking sheets. Grease bottom of small glass; dip in remaining sugar. Press balls to flatten slightly, dipping glass in remaining sugar as necessary.

4. Bake in preheated 375°F oven for 8 to 10 minutes. Remove from sheets; cool completely on wire racks.   *Makes 4$1/2$ dozen*

Preparation Time: 15 minutes
Chill Time: 4 hours
Cook Time: 8 minutes
Total Time: 4 hours and 23 minutes

Peanut Blossoms

1 bag (13 ounces) HERSHEY'S KISSES® Milk Chocolates

$^1/_2$ cup shortening

$^3/_4$ cup REESE'S® Creamy or Crunchy Peanut Butter

$^1/_3$ cup granulated sugar

$^1/_3$ cup packed light brown sugar

1 egg

2 tablespoons milk

1 teaspoon vanilla extract

1$^1/_2$ cups all-purpose flour

1 teaspoon baking soda

$^1/_2$ teaspoon salt

Granulated sugar

1. Heat oven to 375°F. Remove wrappers from chocolate pieces.

2. Beat shortening and peanut butter in large bowl until well blended. Add $^1/_3$ cup granulated sugar and brown sugar; beat until fluffy. Add egg, milk and vanilla; beat well. Stir together flour, baking soda and salt; gradually beat in peanut butter mixture.

3. Shape dough into 1-inch balls. Roll in granulated sugar; place on ungreased cookie sheet.

4. Bake 8 to 10 minutes or until lightly browned. Immediately press a chocolate piece into center of each cookie; cookie will crack around edges. Remove from cookie sheet to wire rack. Cool completely.

Makes about 4 dozen cookies

Chocolate-Dipped Orange Logs

3$\frac{1}{4}$ cups all-purpose flour

$\frac{1}{3}$ teaspoon salt

1 cup butter, softened

1 cup sugar

2 eggs

1$\frac{1}{2}$ teaspoons grated orange peel

1 teaspoon vanilla

1 package (12 ounces) semisweet chocolate chips

1$\frac{1}{2}$ cups pecan pieces, finely chopped

Combine flour and salt in medium bowl. Beat butter in large bowl with electric mixer at medium speed until smooth. Gradually beat in sugar; increase speed to high and beat until light and fluffy. Beat in eggs, 1 at a time, blending well after each addition. Beat in orange peel and vanilla until blended. Gradually stir in flour mixture until blended. (Dough will be crumbly.)

Gather dough together and press gently to form ball. Flatten into disc; wrap in plastic wrap and refrigerate 2 hours or until firm. (Dough can be prepared one day in advance and refrigerated overnight.)

Preheat oven to 350°F. Shape dough into 1-inch balls. Roll balls on flat surface to form 3-inch logs about $\frac{1}{2}$ inch thick. Place logs 1 inch apart on ungreased cookie sheets.

Bake 17 minutes or until bottoms of cookies are golden brown. (Cookies will feel soft and look white on top; they will become crisp when cool.) Transfer to wire racks to cool completely.

Melt chocolate chips in top of double boiler over hot, not boiling, water. Place chopped pecans on sheet of waxed paper. Dip one end of each cookie in chocolate, shaking off excess. Roll chocolate-covered ends in pecans. Place on waxed paper-lined cookie sheets and let stand until chocolate is set, or refrigerate about 5 minutes to set chocolate. Store in airtight container. *Makes about 3 dozen cookies*

Chocolate-Dipped Orange Logs

Chocolate Sugar Spritz

2 squares (1 ounce each) unsweetened chocolate, coarsely chopped

2¼ cups all-purpose flour

¼ teaspoon salt

1 cup butter, softened

¾ cup granulated sugar

1 large egg

1 teaspoon almond extract

½ cup powdered sugar

1 teaspoon ground cinnamon

1. Preheat oven to 400°F.

2. Melt chocolate in small, heavy saucepan over low heat, stirring constantly. Combine flour and salt in small bowl; stir to combine.

3. Beat butter and granulated sugar in large bowl with electric mixer at medium speed until light and fluffy. Beat in egg and almond extract. Beat in chocolate. Gradually add flour mixture with mixing spoon. (Dough will be stiff.)

4. Fit cookie press with desired plate (or change plates for different shapes after first batch). Fill press with dough; press dough 1 inch apart on ungreased cookie sheets.

5. Bake 7 minutes or until just set. Combine powdered sugar and cinnamon in small bowl. Transfer to fine-mesh strainer and sprinkle over hot cookies while they are still on cookie sheets. Remove cookies to wire racks; cool completely.

6. Store tightly covered at room temperature. These cookies do not freeze well.   *Makes 4 to 5 dozen cookies*

Chocolate Sugar Spritz

Banana Crescents

$^{1}/_{2}$ cup chopped almonds, toasted
6 tablespoons sugar, divided
$^{1}/_{2}$ cup margarine, cut into pieces
1$^{1}/_{2}$ cups plus 2 tablespoons all-purpose flour
$^{1}/_{8}$ teaspoon salt
1 extra-ripe, medium DOLE® Banana, peeled
2 to 3 ounces semisweet chocolate chips

• Pulverize almonds with 2 tablespoons sugar.

• Beat margarine, almonds, remaining 4 tablespoons sugar, flour and salt.

• Purée banana; add to almond mixture and mix until well blended.

• Roll tablespoonfuls of dough into logs, then shape into crescents. Place on ungreased cookie sheet. Bake in 375°F oven 25 minutes or until golden. Cool on wire rack.

• Melt chocolate in microwavable dish at MEDIUM (50% power) 1$^{1}/_{2}$ to 2 minutes, stirring once. Dip ends of cookies in chocolate. Refrigerate until chocolate is set.   *Makes 2 dozen cookies*

Banana Crescents

Chocolate Peanut Butter Cup Cookies

COOKIES

1 cup semi-sweet chocolate chips

2 squares (1 ounce each) unsweetened baking chocolate

1 cup sugar

$\frac{1}{2}$ Butter Flavor CRISCO® Stick or $\frac{1}{2}$ cup Butter Flavor CRISCO® all-vegetable shortening

2 eggs

1 teaspoon salt

1 teaspoon vanilla

$1\frac{1}{2}$ cups plus 2 tablespoons all-purpose flour

$\frac{1}{2}$ teaspoon baking soda

$\frac{3}{4}$ cup finely chopped peanuts

36 miniature peanut butter cups, unwrapped

DRIZZLE

1 cup peanut butter chips

1. Heat oven to 350°F. Place sheets of foil on countertop for cooling cookies.

2. For cookies, combine chocolate chips and chocolate squares in microwave-safe measuring cup or bowl. Microwave at 50% power (MEDIUM). Stir after 2 minutes. Repeat until smooth (or melt on rangetop in small saucepan over very low heat). Cool slightly.

3. Combine sugar and $\frac{1}{2}$ cup shortening in large bowl. Beat at medium speed of electric mixer until blended and crumbly. Beat in eggs, one at a time, then salt and vanilla. Reduce speed to low. Add chocolate slowly. Mix

until well blended. Stir in flour and baking soda with spoon until well blended. Shape dough into 1¼-inch balls. Roll in nuts. Place 2 inches apart on ungreased baking sheet.

4. Bake at 350°F for 8 to 10 minutes or until set. *Do not overbake.* Press peanut butter cup into center of each cookie immediately. Press cookie against cup. Cool 2 minutes on baking sheet. Remove cookies to foil to cool completely.

5. For drizzle, place peanut butter chips in heavy resealable sandwich bag. Seal. Microwave at 50% power (MEDIUM). Knead bag after 1 minute. Repeat until smooth (or melt by placing bag in hot water). Cut tiny tip off corner of bag. Squeeze out and drizzle over cookies.

Makes 3 dozen cookies

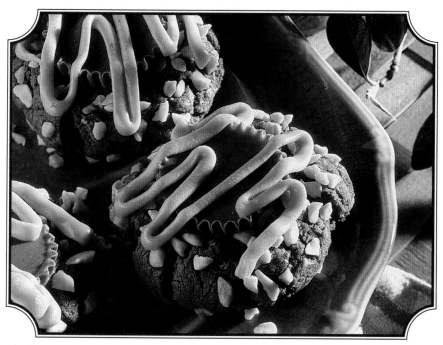

Chocolate Peanut Butter Cup Cookies

Mistletoe Tea Party

Peanut Butter Chip Tassies

Coffee and tea cookies are great for holiday entertaining. So, perk up those poinsettias, straighten the garland, and invite all your friends and family over for a holiday tea party and these great Christmastime cookies.

Peanut Butter Chip Tassies

1 package (3 ounces) cream cheese, softened
$^1/_2$ cup (1 stick) butter, softened
1 cup all-purpose flour
1 egg, slightly beaten
$^1/_2$ cup sugar
2 tablespoons butter, melted
$^1/_4$ teaspoon lemon juice
$^1/_4$ teaspoon vanilla extract
1 cup REESE'S® Peanut Butter Chips, chopped*
6 red candied cherries, quartered (optional)

Do not chop peanut butter chips in food processor or blender.

1. Beat cream cheese and $^1/_2$ cup butter in medium bowl; stir in flour. Cover; refrigerate about one hour or until dough is firm. Shape into 24 one-inch balls; place balls into ungreased, small muffin cups ($1^3/_4$ inches in diameter). Press dough evenly against bottom and sides of each cup.

2. Heat oven to 350°F.

3. Combine egg, sugar, melted butter, lemon juice and vanilla in medium bowl; stir until smooth. Add chopped peanut butter chips. Fill muffin cups $^3/_4$ full with mixture.

4. Bake 20 to 25 minutes or until filling is set and lightly browned. Cool completely; remove from pan to wire rack. Garnish with candied cherries, if desired.   *Makes about 2 dozen tassies*

Florentine Cookies

¼ cup unsalted butter

¼ cup sugar

1 tablespoon heavy or whipping cream

¼ cup sliced blanched almonds, finely chopped

¼ cup walnuts, finely chopped

5 red candied cherries, finely chopped

1 tablespoon golden or dark raisins, finely chopped

1 tablespoon crystallized ginger, finely chopped

1 tablespoon diced candied lemon peel, finely chopped

3 tablespoons all-purpose flour

4 ounces semisweet chocolate, chopped

1. Preheat oven to 350°F. Grease 2 large baking sheets.

2. Combine butter, sugar and cream in small heavy saucepan. Cook, uncovered, over medium heat until sugar dissolves and mixture boils, stirring constantly. Cook and stir 1 minute more; remove from heat. Stir in nuts, fruit, ginger and lemon peel. Add flour; mix well.

3. Spoon heaping teaspoonfuls batter onto prepared baking sheets. Repeat, placing 4 cookies on each baking sheet to allow room for spreading.

4. Bake cookies, 1 baking sheet at a time, 8 to 10 minutes or until deep brown. Remove baking sheet from oven to wire rack. (If cookies have spread unevenly, push in edges with metal spatula to round out shape.) Cool cookies 1 minute or until firm enough to remove from sheet; then quickly and carefully remove cookies to wire racks. Cool completely.

5. Repeat with remaining batter. (To prevent cookies from spreading too quickly, allow baking sheets to cool before greasing and spooning batter onto sheets.)

6. Bring water in bottom of double boiler just to a boil; remove from heat. Place chocolate in top of double boiler and place over water. Stir chocolate until melted; immediately remove top of double boiler from water. Let chocolate cool slightly.

7. Line large baking sheets with waxed paper. Turn cookies over; spread chocolate on bottoms. Place cookies, chocolate side up, on prepared baking sheets; let stand until chocolate is almost set. Score chocolate in zig-zag pattern with tines of fork. Let stand until completely set or refrigerate until firm. Serve, or store in airtight container in refrigerator.

Makes about 2 dozen cookies

Florentine Cookies

Mocha Biscotti

2 1/2 cups all-purpose flour

1/2 cup unsweetened cocoa

2 teaspoons baking powder

1 1/4 cups sugar

3/4 cup egg substitute

1/4 cup margarine or butter, melted

4 teaspoons instant coffee powder

1/2 teaspoon vanilla extract

1/3 cup PLANTERS® Slivered Almonds, chopped

Powdered sugar, optional

1. Mix flour, cocoa and baking powder in small bowl; set aside.

2. Beat sugar, egg substitute, melted margarine or butter, coffee powder and vanilla in large bowl with mixer at medium speed for 2 minutes. Stir in flour mixture and almonds.

3. Divide dough in half. With floured hands, shape each portion of dough into 14×2-inch log on a greased baking sheet. (Dough will be sticky.) Bake in preheated 350°F oven for 25 minutes.

4. Remove from oven and cut each log on a diagonal into 16 (1-inch) slices. Place biscotti, cut-side up, on baking sheets; return to oven and bake 10 to 15 minutes more on each side or until lightly toasted.

5. Remove from sheets. Cool completely on wire racks. Dust biscotti tops with powdered sugar if desired.   *Makes 32 biscotti*

Preparation Time: 20 minutes

Cook Time: 35 minutes

Total Time: 1 hour and 5 minutes

Mocha Biscotti

Kolacky

$^1/_2$ cup margarine or butter, softened

3 ounces cream cheese, softened

1 teaspoon vanilla

1 cup all-purpose flour

$^1/_8$ teaspoon salt

$^1/_4$ cup all-fruit spread, assorted flavors

1 egg

1 teaspoon cold water

Combine margarine and cream cheese in large bowl; beat with electric mixer at medium speed until smooth and creamy. Beat in vanilla. Combine flour and salt in small bowl; gradually add to margarine mixture, beating until mixture forms soft dough. Divide dough in half; wrap each half in plastic wrap. Refrigerate until firm.

Preheat oven to 375°F.

Roll out half of dough on lightly floured pastry cloth or board to $^1/_8$-inch thickness. Cut with 3-inch round cookie cutter. Beat egg with water in small bowl; lightly brush onto dough circles. Spoon $^1/_2$ teaspoon fruit spread onto center of each dough circle. Bring three edges of dough up over fruit spread; pinch edges together to seal. Place on ungreased cookie sheets; brush with egg mixture. Repeat with remaining dough and fruit spread.

Bake 12 minutes or until golden brown. Let stand on cookie sheets 1 minute. Transfer cookies to wire racks; cool completely. Store in tightly covered container.   *Makes 2 dozen kolacky*

Kolacky

Cappuccino Cookies

1¼ cups firmly packed light brown sugar

1 Butter Flavor CRISCO® Stick or 1 cup Butter Flavor
CRISCO® all-vegetable shortening

2 eggs

¼ cup light corn syrup or regular pancake syrup

2 tablespoons instant espresso or coffee powder

1 teaspoon vanilla

1 teaspoon rum extract

3 cups all-purpose flour

¾ teaspoon baking powder

½ teaspoon *each* baking soda, salt and nutmeg

Chocolate jimmies

1. Place brown sugar and shortening in large bowl. Beat at medium speed of electric mixer until well blended. Add eggs, corn syrup, coffee, vanilla, and rum extract; beat until well blended and fluffy.

2. Combine flour, baking powder, baking soda, salt and nutmeg. Add gradually to shortening mixture, beating at low speed until blended. Divide dough in half. Roll each half into two logs approximately 2 inches in diameter. Wrap in waxed paper. Refrigerate several hours.

3. Heat oven to 350°F. Place sheets of foil on countertop for cooling cookies. Cut cookies into ¼-inch-thick slices. Place 2 inches apart on ungreased baking sheet. Sprinkle center of each cookie with jimmies.

4. Bake one baking sheet at a time at 350°F for 10 to 12 minutes or until golden brown. *Do not overbake.* Cool 2 minutes on baking sheet. Remove cookies to foil to cool completely.

Makes about 4½ dozen cookies

Butter Pecan Crisps

1 cup unsalted butter, softened

$^3/_4$ cup granulated sugar

$^3/_4$ cup packed brown sugar

$^1/_2$ teaspoon salt

2 eggs

1 teaspoon vanilla

1$^1/_2$ cups finely ground pecans

2$^1/_2$ cups sifted all-purpose flour

1 teaspoon baking soda

30 pecan halves

4 squares (1 ounce each) semisweet chocolate

1 tablespoon shortening

Preheat oven to 375°F. Beat butter, sugars and salt in large bowl until light and fluffy. Add eggs, 1 at a time, beating well after each addition. Beat in vanilla and ground pecans. Combine flour and baking soda in small bowl. Gradually stir flour mixture into butter mixture. Spoon dough into large pastry bag fitted with $^3/_8$-inch round tip; fill bag halfway. Shake down dough to remove air bubbles. Hold bag perpendicular to, and about $^1/_2$ inch above, parchment paper-lined cookie sheets. Pipe dough into 1$^1/_4$-inch balls, spacing 3 inches apart. Cut each pecan half lengthwise into 2 slivers. Press 1 sliver in center of each dough ball.

Bake 9 to 12 minutes or until lightly browned. Cool 5 minutes on cookie sheets. Remove to wire racks; cool completely. Melt chocolate and shortening in small heavy saucepan over low heat; stir to blend. Drizzle chocolate mixture over cookies. Let stand until chocolate is set.

Makes about 5 dozen cookies

Marvelous Macaroons

1 can (8 ounces) DOLE® Crushed Pineapple

1 can (14 ounces) sweetened condensed milk

1 package (7 ounces) flaked coconut

$^1/_2$ cup margarine, melted

$^1/_2$ cup chopped almonds, toasted

1 teaspoon grated lemon peel

$^1/_4$ teaspoon almond extract

1 cup all-purpose flour

1 teaspoon baking powder

• Preheat oven to 350°F. Drain pineapple well, pressing out excess juice with back of spoon. In large bowl, combine drained pineapple, milk, coconut, margarine, almonds, lemon peel and almond extract.

• In small bowl, combine flour and baking powder. Beat into pineapple mixture until blended. Drop heaping tablespoonfuls of dough 1 inch apart onto greased cookie sheets.

• Bake 13 to 15 minutes or until lightly browned. Garnish with whole almonds, if desired. Cool on wire racks. Store in covered container in refrigerator. *Makes about 3$^1/_2$ dozen cookies*

Marvelous Macaroons

Classic Anise Biscotti

4 ounces whole blanched almonds (about $^3/_4$ cup)

$2^1/_4$ cups all-purpose flour

1 teaspoon baking powder

$^3/_4$ teaspoon salt

$^3/_4$ cup sugar

$^1/_2$ cup unsalted butter, softened

3 eggs

2 tablespoons brandy

2 teaspoons grated lemon peel

1 tablespoon whole anise seeds

1. Preheat oven to 375°F. To toast almonds, spread on baking sheet. Bake 6 to 8 minutes or until toasted and light brown; turn off oven. Remove almonds to cutting board; cool. Coarsely chop.

2. Combine flour, baking powder and salt in small bowl. Beat sugar and butter in medium bowl with electric mixer at medium speed until light and fluffy. Add eggs, 1 at a time, beating well after each addition and scraping side of bowl often. Stir in brandy and lemon peel. Add flour mixture gradually; stir until smooth. Stir in chopped almonds and anise seeds. Cover and refrigerate dough 1 hour or until firm.

3. Preheat oven to 375°F. Grease large baking sheet. Divide dough in half. Shape $^1/_2$ of dough into 12×2-inch log on lightly floured surface. (Dough will be fairly soft.) Pat smooth with lightly floured fingertips. Transfer to prepared baking sheet. Repeat with remaining $^1/_2$ of dough to form second log. Bake 20 to 25 minutes or until logs are light golden brown. Remove baking sheet from oven to wire rack; turn off oven. Cool logs completely.

4. Preheat oven to 350°F. Cut logs diagonally with serrated knife into ¹⁄₂-inch-thick slices. Place slices flat in single layer on 2 ungreased baking sheets.

5. Bake 8 minutes. Turn slices over; bake 10 to 12 minutes or until cut surfaces are light brown and cookies are dry. Remove cookies to wire racks; cool completely. Store cookies in airtight container up to 2 weeks.

Makes about 4 dozen biscotti

Classic Anise Biscotti

Spiced Wafers

$^1/_2$ cup butter, softened

1 cup sugar

1 egg

2 tablespoons milk

1 teaspoon vanilla

1$^3/_4$ cups all-purpose flour

2 teaspoons baking powder

1 teaspoon ground cinnamon

$^1/_2$ teaspoon ground nutmeg

$^1/_4$ teaspoon ground cloves

Red hot candies or red colored sugar for garnish (optional)

Beat butter in large bowl with electric mixer at medium speed until smooth. Add sugar; beat until well blended. Add egg, milk and vanilla; beat until well blended.

Combine flour, baking powder, cinnamon, nutmeg and cloves in large bowl. Gradually add flour mixture to butter mixture at low speed, blending well after each addition.

Shape dough into 2 logs, each about 2 inches in diameter and 6 inches long. Wrap each log in plastic wrap. Refrigerate 2 to 3 hours or overnight.

Preheat oven to 350°F. Grease cookie sheets. Cut logs into $^1/_4$-inch-thick slices; decorate with candies or colored sugar, if desired. (Or leave plain and decorate with icing later.) Place at least 2 inches apart on cookie sheets.

Bake 11 to 13 minutes or until edges are light brown. Transfer to wire racks to cool. Store in airtight container.   *Makes about 4 dozen cookies*

Spiced Wafers

Chocolate Almond Biscotti

1 package DUNCAN HINES® Moist Deluxe® Dark Chocolate
   Cake Mix
1 cup all-purpose flour
$^{1}/_{2}$ cup (1 stick) butter or margarine, melted
2 eggs
1 teaspoon almond extract
$^{1}/_{2}$ cup chopped almonds
   White chocolate, melted (optional)

Preheat oven to 350°F. Line 2 baking sheets with parchment paper.

Combine cake mix, flour, butter, eggs and almond extract in large bowl.
Beat at low speed with electric mixer until well blended; stir in nuts.
Divide dough in half. Shape each half into a 12×2-inch log; place logs
on prepared baking sheets. (Bake logs separately.)

Bake 30 to 35 minutes or until toothpick inserted in center comes out
clean. Remove logs from oven; cool on baking sheets 15 minutes. Using
serrated knife, cut logs into $^{1}/_{2}$-inch slices. Arrange slices on baking
sheets. Bake biscotti 10 minutes. Remove to cooling racks; cool
completely.

Dip one end of each biscotti in melted white chocolate, if desired. Allow
white chocolate to set at room temperature before storing biscotti in
airtight container.   *Makes about 2$^{1}/_{2}$ dozen cookies*

Chocolate Almond Biscotti

Welsh Tea Cakes

$^{3}/_{4}$ cup chopped dried mixed fruit or fruit bits or golden raisins

2 tablespoons brandy or cognac

$2^{1}/_{4}$ cups all-purpose flour

$2^{1}/_{2}$ teaspoons ground cinnamon, divided

1 teaspoon baking powder

$^{1}/_{2}$ teaspoon baking soda

$^{1}/_{4}$ teaspoon salt

$^{1}/_{4}$ teaspoon ground cloves

1 cup butter, softened

$1^{1}/_{4}$ cups sugar, divided

1 egg

$^{1}/_{3}$ cup sliced almonds (optional)

1. Preheat oven to 375°F. Combine dried fruit and brandy in medium bowl; let sit at least 10 minutes to plump.

2. Place flour, $1^{1}/_{2}$ teaspoons cinnamon, baking powder, baking soda, salt and cloves in medium bowl; stir to combine.

3. Beat butter and 1 cup sugar in large bowl until light and fluffy. Beat in egg. Gradually add flour mixture. Beat until well blended. Stir in fruit and brandy mixture with spoon.

4. Combine remaining $^{1}/_{4}$ cup sugar and 1 teaspoon cinnamon in small bowl. Shape heaping teaspoonfuls of dough into 1-inch balls; roll balls in cinnamon-sugar to coat. Place balls 2 inches apart on ungreased cookie sheets.

5. Press balls to $^{1}/_{4}$-inch thickness using bottom of glass dipped in granulated sugar. Press 3 almond slices horizontally into center of each cookie, if desired. (Almonds will spread evenly and flatten upon baking.)

6. Bake 10 to 12 minutes or until lightly browned. Remove tea cakes to wire racks; cool completely. Store tightly covered at room temperature or freeze up to 3 months. *Makes about 3½ dozen cookies*

Welsh Tea Cakes

Worldwide Yuletide Favorites

Pfeffernüsse

Santa's picked up a thing or two in his worldwide travels; the reindeer think he's the international cookie connoisseur. Here is a selection of his holiday favorites from around the world.

Pfeffernüsse

3 1/2 cups all-purpose flour

2 teaspoons baking powder

1 1/2 teaspoons ground cinnamon

1 teaspoon ground ginger

1/2 teaspoon baking soda

1/2 teaspoon salt

1/2 teaspoon ground cloves

1/2 teaspoon ground cardamom

1/4 teaspoon black pepper

1 cup butter, softened

1 cup granulated sugar

1/4 cup dark molasses

1 egg

Powdered sugar

Combine flour, baking powder, cinnamon, ginger, baking soda, salt, cloves, cardamom and pepper in large bowl. Beat butter and granulated sugar in large bowl with electric mixer at medium speed until light and fluffy. Beat in molasses and egg. Gradually add flour mixture. Beat at low speed until dough forms. Shape dough into disk; wrap in plastic wrap and refrigerate until firm, 30 minutes or up to 3 days.

Preheat oven to 350°F. Grease cookie sheets. Roll dough into 1-inch balls. Place 2 inches apart on prepared cookie sheets.

Bake 12 to 14 minutes or until golden brown. Transfer cookies to wire racks; dust with sifted powdered sugar. Cool completely. Store tightly covered at room temperature or freeze up to 3 months.

Makes about 5 dozen cookies

Mexican Chocolate Macaroons

1 package (8 ounces) semisweet baking chocolate, divided

1¾ cups plus ⅓ cup whole almonds, divided

¾ cup sugar

1 teaspoon ground cinnamon

1 teaspoon vanilla

2 egg whites

1. Preheat oven to 400°F. Grease baking sheets; set aside.

2. Place 5 squares chocolate in food processor; process until coarsely chopped. Add 1¾ cups almonds and sugar; process using on/off pulsing action until mixture is finely ground. Add cinnamon, vanilla and egg whites; process just until mixture forms moist dough.

3. Form dough into 1-inch balls (dough will be sticky). Place about 2 inches apart on prepared baking sheets. Press 1 almond on top of each cookie.

4. Bake 8 to 10 minutes or just until set. Cool 2 minutes on baking sheets. Remove cookies from baking sheets to wire racks. Cool completely.

5. Heat remaining 3 squares chocolate in small saucepan over very low heat until melted. Spoon chocolate into small resealable plastic food storage bag. Cut small corner off bottom of bag with scissors. Drizzle chocolate over cookies. *Makes 3 dozen cookies*

Tip: For longer storage, allow cookies to stand until chocolate drizzle is set. Store in airtight containers.

Prep and Bake Time: 30 minutes

Mexican Chocolate Macaroons

Fried Norwegian Cookies

2 large eggs, at room temperature
3 tablespoons granulated sugar
$^1/_4$ cup butter, melted
2 tablespoons milk
1 teaspoon vanilla
$1^3/_4$ to 2 cups all-purpose flour
Vegetable oil
Powdered sugar

Beat eggs and granulated sugar in large bowl with electric mixer at medium speed until thick and lemon colored. Beat in butter, milk and vanilla until well blended. Gradually add $1^1/_2$ cups flour. Beat at low speed until well blended. Stir in enough remaining flour with spoon to form soft dough. Divide dough into 4 portions; cover and refrigerate until firm, at least 2 hours or overnight.

Working with floured hands, shape 1 portion dough at a time into 1-inch-thick square. Place dough on lightly floured surface. Roll out dough to 11-inch square. Cut dough into $1^1/_4$-inch strips; cut strips diagonally at 2-inch intervals. Cut $1^1/_4$-inch slit vertically down center of each strip. Insert one end of strip through cut to form twist; repeat with each strip. Repeat with remaining dough portions.

Heat oil in large saucepan to 365°F. Place 12 cookies at a time in hot oil. Fry about $1^1/_2$ minutes or until golden brown, turning cookies once with slotted spoon. Drain on paper towels. Dust cookies with powdered sugar. Cookies are best if served immediately, but can be stored in airtight container for up to 1 day. *Makes about 11 dozen cookies*

Fried Norwegian Cookies

Moravian Spice Crisps

$^1/_3$ cup shortening

$^1/_3$ cup packed brown sugar

$^1/_4$ cup unsulfured molasses

$^1/_4$ cup dark corn syrup

1$^3/_4$ to 2 cups all-purpose flour

2 teaspoons ground ginger

1$^1/_4$ teaspoons baking soda

1 teaspoon ground cinnamon

$^1/_2$ teaspoon ground cloves

Powdered sugar

1. Melt shortening in small saucepan over low heat. Remove from heat; stir in brown sugar, molasses and corn syrup. Set aside; cool.

2. Place 1$^1/_2$ cups flour, ginger, baking soda, cinnamon and cloves in large bowl; stir to combine. Beat in shortening mixture. Gradually beat in remaining $^1/_4$ cup flour to form stiff dough.

3. Knead dough on lightly floured surface, adding more flour if too sticky. Form dough into 2 discs; wrap in plastic wrap and refrigerate 30 minutes or until firm.

4. Preheat oven to 350°F. Grease cookie sheets; set aside. Working with 1 disc at a time, roll out dough on lightly floured surface to $^1/_{16}$-inch thickness.

5. Cut dough with floured 2$^3/_8$-inch scalloped cookie cutter. (If dough becomes too soft, refrigerate several minutes before continuing.) Gently press dough trimmings together; reroll and cut out more cookies. Place cutouts $^1/_2$ inch apart on prepared cookie sheets.

6. Bake 8 minutes or until firm. Remove cookies to wire racks; cool completely.

7. Place small strips of cardboard or parchment paper over cookies; dust with sifted powdered sugar. Carefully remove cardboard.

Makes about 6 dozen cookies

Moravian Spice Crisps

111

Belgian Tuile Cookies

$^{1}/_{2}$ cup butter, softened

$^{1}/_{2}$ cup sugar

1 egg white

1 teaspoon vanilla

$^{1}/_{4}$ teaspoon salt

$^{1}/_{2}$ cup all-purpose flour

4 ounces bittersweet chocolate, chopped, or semisweet chocolate chips

1. Preheat oven to 375°F. Grease cookie sheets; set aside.

2. Beat butter and sugar in large bowl until light and fluffy. Beat in egg white, vanilla and salt. Gradually add flour. Beat until well blended. Drop rounded teaspoonfuls of batter 4 inches apart onto prepared cookie sheets. (Bake only 4 cookies per sheet.) Flatten slightly with spatula.

3. Bake 6 to 8 minutes or until cookies are deep golden brown. Let cookies stand on cookie sheet 1 minute. Working quickly while cookies are still hot, drape cookies over rolling pin or bottle so both sides hang down and form saddle shape; cool completely.

4. Melt chocolate in small heavy saucepan over low heat, stirring constantly.

5. Tilt saucepan to pool chocolate at one end; dip edge of each cookie, turning slowly so entire edge is tinged with chocolate.

6. Transfer cookies to waxed paper; let stand at room temperature 1 hour or until set. Store tightly covered at room temperature. Do not freeze.

Makes about 2$^{1}/_{2}$ dozen cookies

Belgian Tuile Cookies

Danish Lemon-Filled Spice Cookies

2¼ cups all-purpose flour

1 teaspoon ground cinnamon

½ teaspoon ground allspice

½ teaspoon ground ginger

½ teaspoon ground nutmeg

¼ teaspoon salt

¾ cup butter, softened

¾ cup sugar

¼ cup milk

1 egg yolk

1 teaspoon vanilla

Additional sugar

Lemon Filling (recipe follows)

Place flour, cinnamon, allspice, ginger, nutmeg and salt in medium bowl; stir to combine. Beat butter, ¾ cup sugar, milk, egg yolk and vanilla in large bowl. Beat butter mixture with electric mixer at medium speed until light and fluffy. Gradually add flour mixture. Beat at low speed until dough forms. Cover dough and refrigerate 30 minutes or until firm.

Preheat oven to 350°F. Grease cookie sheets. Shape teaspoonfuls of dough into ½-inch balls; place 2 inches apart on prepared cookie sheets. Flatten each ball to ¼-inch thickness with bottom of glass dipped in sugar. Prick top of each cookie using fork. Bake 10 to 13 minutes or until golden brown. Remove cookies to wire racks; cool completely.

Prepare Lemon Filling. Spread filling on flat side of half of cookies. Top with remaining cookies, pressing flat sides together. Let stand at room temperature until set. Store tightly covered at room temperature or freeze up to 3 months.   *Makes about 3 dozen sandwich cookies*

Lemon Filling

2$1/4$ cups sifted powdered sugar
3 tablespoons lemon juice
1$1/2$ tablespoons butter, softened
$1/2$ teaspoon lemon extract

Beat all ingredients in medium bowl with electric mixer at medium speed until smooth.   *Makes about 1 cup*

Scottish Shortbread

5 cups all-purpose flour
1 cup rice flour
2 cups butter, softened
1 cup sugar
Candied fruit (optional)

Preheat oven to 325°F. Sift together flours. Beat butter and sugar in large bowl with electric mixer at medium speed until creamy. Blend in $3/4$ of flour until mixture resembles fine crumbs. Stir in remaining flour by hand. Press dough firmly into ungreased 15$1/2$×10$1/2$×1-inch jelly-roll pan or two 9-inch fluted tart pans; crimp and flute edges of dough in jelly-roll pan, if desired. Bake 40 to 45 minutes or until light brown. Place pan on wire rack. Cut into bars or wedges while warm. Decorate with candied fruit, if desired. Cool completely. Store in airtight containers.

Makes about 4 dozen bars or 24 wedges

Argentinean Caramel-Filled Pasteles

3 cups all-purpose flour

1/2 cup powdered sugar

1 teaspoon baking powder

1/4 teaspoon salt

1 cup butter, cut into small pieces

6 to 7 tablespoons ice water

1/2 package (14 ounces) caramel candies, unwrapped

2 tablespoons milk

1/2 cup flaked coconut

1 egg

1 tablespoon water

Combine flour, sugar, baking powder and salt in large bowl. Cut butter into flour mixture with 2 knives until crumbly. Add water, 1 tablespoon at a time; toss with fork until mixture holds together. Divide dough in half; cover. Refrigerate 30 minutes or until firm.

Meanwhile, melt caramels and milk in medium saucepan over low heat, stirring constantly; stir in coconut. Remove from heat; cool.

On lightly floured surface, roll out each dough portion to 1/8-inch thickness. Cut with 3-inch round cookie cutter. Repeat with trimmings.

Preheat oven to 400°F. Grease cookie sheets; set aside. Beat egg and water in cup. Place 1/2 teaspoon caramel mixture in center of each dough round. Moisten edge of dough round with egg mixture. Fold dough in half; press edges with fork to firmly seal in filling. Place on prepared cookie sheets; brush with egg mixture. Cut 3 slashes across top of each cookie with tip of knife. Bake 15 to 20 minutes or until golden brown. Remove cookies to wire racks to cool. *Makes about 4 dozen cookies*

116

Argentinean Caramel-Filled Pasteles

117

Viennese Hazelnut Butter Thins

1 cup hazelnuts
$1^1/_4$ cups all-purpose flour
$^1/_4$ teaspoon salt
$1^1/_4$ cups powdered sugar
1 cup butter, softened
1 egg
1 teaspoon vanilla
1 cup semisweet chocolate chips

1. Preheat oven to 350°F. To remove skins from hazelnuts, spread in single layer on baking sheet. Bake 10 to 12 minutes or until toasted and skins begin to flake off; let cool slightly. Wrap hazelnuts in heavy kitchen towel; rub against towel to remove as much of the skins as possible.

2. Place hazelnuts in food processor. Process using on/off pulsing action until hazelnuts are ground but not pasty.

3. Combine flour and salt in small bowl. Beat powdered sugar and butter in medium bowl with electric mixer at medium speed until light and fluffy. Beat in egg and vanilla. Gradually add flour mixture. Beat in ground hazelnuts at low speed until well blended.

4. Place dough on sheet of waxed paper. Using waxed paper to hold dough, roll back and forth to form log 12 inches long and $2^1/_2$ inches wide. Wrap log in plastic wrap; refrigerate until firm, at least 2 hours or up to 48 hours.

5. Preheat oven to 350°F. Cut dough into $^1/_4$-inch-thick slices; place on *ungreased* cookie sheets.

6. Bake 10 to 12 minutes or until edges are very lightly browned. Let cookies stand on cookie sheets 1 minute. Remove cookies to wire racks; cool completely.

7. Place chocolate chips in 2-cups microwavable glass measure. Place in microwave and heat on HIGH 1 to 1$\frac{1}{2}$ minutes or until melted, stirring after 1 minute and at 30-second intervals after first minute.

8. Dip cookies into chocolate, coating about $\frac{1}{2}$ of each cookie. Let excess drip back into cup. Transfer cookies to waxed paper; let stand at room temperature 1 hour or until set. *Makes about 3 dozen cookies*

Note: To store cookies, place in airtight container between layers of waxed paper. Cookies can be frozen for up to 3 months.

Viennese Hazelnut Butter Thins

119

Linzer Sandwich Cookies

1⅓ cups all-purpose flour

¼ teaspoon baking powder

¼ teaspoon salt

¾ cup granulated sugar

½ cup butter, softened

1 large egg

1 teaspoon vanilla

Powdered sugar (optional)

Seedless raspberry jam

Place flour, baking powder and salt in small bowl; stir to combine. Beat granulated sugar and butter in medium bowl with electric mixer at medium speed until light and fluffy. Beat in egg and vanilla. Gradually add flour mixture. Beat at low speed until dough forms. Divide dough in half; cover and refrigerate 2 hours or until firm.

Preheat oven to 375°F. Working with 1 portion at a time, roll out dough on lightly floured surface to 3/16-inch thickness. Cut dough into desired shapes with floured cookie cutters. Cut out equal numbers of each shape. (If dough becomes too soft, refrigerate several minutes before continuing.) Cut 1-inch centers out of half the cookies of each shape. Reroll trimmings and cut out more cookies. Place cookies 1½ to 2 inches apart on ungreased cookie sheets. Bake 7 to 9 minutes or until edges are lightly brown. Let cookies stand on cookie sheets 1 to 2 minutes. Remove cookies to wire racks; cool completely.

Sprinkle cookies with holes with powdered sugar, if desired. Spread 1 teaspoon jam on flat side of whole cookies, spreading almost to edges. Place cookies with holes, flat side down, over jam.

Makes about 2 dozen sandwich cookies

Linzer Sandwich Cookies

ACKNOWLEDGMENTS

The publisher would like to thank the companies and organizations listed below for the use of their recipes and photographs in this publication.

California Dried Plum Board

Dole Food Company, Inc.

Duncan Hines® and Moist Deluxe® are registered trademarks of Aurora Foods Inc.

Fleischmann's® Original Spread

Hershey Foods Corporation

Kraft Foods Holdings

© Mars, Incorporated 2002

Mott's® is a registered trademark of Mott's, Inc.

Nestlé USA

PLANTERS® Nuts

The Procter & Gamble Company

Unilever Bestfoods North America

Wisconsin Milk Marketing Board

122

METRIC CONVERSION CHART

VOLUME MEASUREMENTS (dry)

1/8 teaspoon = 0.5 mL
1/4 teaspoon = 1 mL
1/2 teaspoon = 2 mL
3/4 teaspoon = 4 mL
1 teaspoon = 5 mL
1 tablespoon = 15 mL
2 tablespoons = 30 mL
1/4 cup = 60 mL
1/3 cup = 75 mL
1/2 cup = 125 mL
2/3 cup = 150 mL
3/4 cup = 175 mL
1 cup = 250 mL
2 cups = 1 pint = 500 mL
3 cups = 750 mL
4 cups = 1 quart = 1 L

VOLUME MEASUREMENTS (fluid)

1 fluid ounce (2 tablespoons) = 30 mL
4 fluid ounces (1/2 cup) = 125 mL
8 fluid ounces (1 cup) = 250 mL
12 fluid ounces (1 1/2 cups) = 375 mL
16 fluid ounces (2 cups) = 500 mL

WEIGHTS (mass)

1/2 ounce = 15 g
1 ounce = 30 g
3 ounces = 90 g
4 ounces = 120 g
8 ounces = 225 g
10 ounces = 285 g
12 ounces = 360 g
16 ounces = 1 pound = 450 g

DIMENSIONS

1/16 inch = 2 mm
1/8 inch = 3 mm
1/4 inch = 6 mm
1/2 inch = 1.5 cm
3/4 inch = 2 cm
1 inch = 2.5 cm

OVEN TEMPERATURES

250°F = 120°C
275°F = 140°C
300°F = 150°C
325°F = 160°C
350°F = 180°C
375°F = 190°C
400°F = 200°C
425°F = 220°C
450°F = 230°C

BAKING PAN SIZES

Utensil	Size in Inches/Quarts	Metric Volume	Size in Centimeters
Baking or Cake Pan (square or rectangular)	8×8×2	2 L	20×20×5
	9×9×2	2.5 L	23×23×5
	12×8×2	3 L	30×20×5
	13×9×2	3.5 L	33×23×5
Loaf Pan	8×4×3	1.5 L	20×10×7
	9×5×3	2 L	23×13×7
Round Layer Cake Pan	8×1½	1.2 L	20×4
	9×1½	1.5 L	23×4
Pie Plate	8×1¼	750 mL	20×3
	9×1¼	1 L	23×3
Baking Dish or Casserole	1 quart	1 L	—
	1½ quart	1.5 L	—
	2 quart	2 L	—